WOMEN
IN HISTORY

WOMEN AND TRAVEL

Dea Birkett

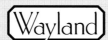

WOMEN
IN HISTORY

Women and the Arts
Women and Business
Women and Education
Women and the Family
Women and Literature
Women and the Media
Women and Politics
Women and Science
Women and Sport
Women and War
Women and Work

Editor: Catherine Ellis
Designer: Nick Cannan

Front cover: Jean Batten, about to embark on her solo return flight from Sydney to England, 1935.

Back cover: Top left – Mary Douglas, anthropologist. Top right – a medieval drawing of the Wife of Bath, from Chaucer's *Canterbury Tales*. Bottom left – Lady Dorothy Mills in West Africa. Bottom right – a traveller being lowered over the side of a ship in a 'mammy' chair. Surf boats wait to take her to the African shore.

First published in 1991 by
Wayland (Publishers) Limited
61 Western Road, Hove
East Sussex BN3 1JD, England

British Library Cataloguing in Publication Data
Birkett, Dea
    Women and travel. – (Women in history)
    I. Title   II. Series
    910.82

    ISBN 0–7502–0160–6

Typeset by Kalligraphic Design Ltd, Horley, Surrey
Printed in Italy by G. Canale & C.S.p.A., Turin
Bound in France by A.G.M.

Picture acknowledgements
The pictures in this book were supplied by the following: Australian Overseas Information Service, London 32 (both); Dea Birkett Back cover bottom left, 4, 25 (both), 29; Mary Evans Picture Library Back cover top right, 9 (both), 22, 24 (bottom), 26; Eye Ubiquitous 38; Lady Faber 35; Hulton Picture Company Front cover, 10, 13, 14; Liverpool City Council, Libraries and Arts Dept. Back cover bottom right; Billie Love 17, 19, 21, 23, 24 (top); The Mansell Collection 7, 11, 18; Christine Osborne 43; Photri 15, 16, 30 (left); Rex Features 44; Royal Geographical Society 31; Royal Anthropological Institute Back cover top left, 30 (right); Ronald Sheridan's Photo Library 5, 8; Topham Picture Library 34, 36, 37, 39, 42; Terry Tullis 40 (both). The map artwork was supplied by Peter Bull.

Contents

Lady Dorothy Mills was the first English woman to visit the legendary city of Timbuktu, in 1923. She wrote many books about her travels through Africa.

Introduction

The saying 'A woman's place is in the home' is well known, but for many centuries women have travelled far away from their families and friends. They have undertaken their journeys for many different reasons. Some were motivated by religious inspiration to become pilgrims and missionaries. Others were forced to leave their homes through poverty, and look for a better life abroad. A few women had enough money to travel simply for the fun of it. Many went to Africa and Asia as professional anthropologists.

For many women these professional and economic motives hid a deeper spur. Women over the centuries have been driven to travel by a feeling that their home society did not allow them to do what they really wanted to. Far away from the pressures of family and the role expected of her, a woman often found a new sense of freedom in travelling. In the desert, on the mountainside, or deep in a tropical forest, she could throw off all the manners of her home and just be herself.

Many of the stories of the women who travelled far away have been hidden for a long time. Few people know that the famous nineteenth-century explorer David Livingstone travelled with his wife Mary, who died and was buried in Africa. Other women who travelled alone and even published accounts of their experiences have since been forgotten. The first known travel account is by the Abbess Egeria in AD 383, but it was not discovered until 1500 years later in 1884.

Today, more and more of these stories are available. How women see and write about a far off people and land is considered important. Some women travellers claim special insights on the grounds of their sex. They argue that they can understand and report on foreign women and home-life in a way no male traveller can. Other women travellers seek to be accepted on equal terms with men, claiming they have the same outlook and attitudes.

1

Pilgrims

AD 300–1600

In Europe in medieval times, from the fourth to the fifteenth centuries, the main reason for making a journey was to go on a pilgrimage. Many of these Christian travellers were women. As early as AD 381, an abbess called Egeria went on a three-year pilgrimage from France to the Holy Lands of Palestine and Egypt. Like other pilgrims, Egeria was far more interested in the ancient monuments and places associated with the Bible than the people she met and lands she travelled through. She used her Bible as her guidebook, visiting places mentioned in it such as the burning bush, Bethlehem, and Mount Sinai where Moses is supposed to have received the Commandments from God. The account of her travels is the first known travel account by a woman.

Santiago de Compostela in Northern Spain was the most popular destination for European pilgrims. There is a shrine to St James there.

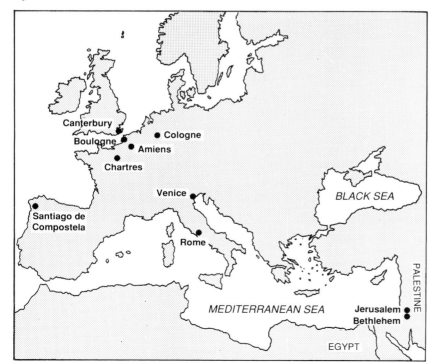

This map shows some of the holy places in Europe to which pilgrimages were commonly made between AD 300–1500.

'

Nothing could hold her back, whether it was the labour of travelling the whole world . . . the perils of the sea and rivers . . . the dread crags and fearsome mountains.
Seventh century monk Valerius on the Abbess Egeria, the first known woman travel writer.

'

It would be well and favourable . . . if your synod would forbid matrons and veiled women to make these frequent journeys back and forth to Rome.
St Boniface to the Archbishop of Canterbury, eighth century.

A medieval pilgrimage was undertaken for religious devotion or as a penance to make up for sins committed. In the fifth century, St Marcianus persuaded a group of former prostitutes to prove that they had truly repented by making a pilgrimage to Jerusalem. Two hundred years later, the route to the East from Europe was so well trod that pilgrims could buy guides with titles such as *Description of the Holy Land* and *Information for Pilgrims*. These recommended churches to be visited, where to stay, and gave road and river conditions. Cheap souvenirs were for sale along the way. At Amiens Cathedral in northern France, where the skull of John the Baptist was said to be stored, a pilgrim could buy a brooch representing John the Baptist's head. By the fifteenth century, all-in packages could be taken from Venice to the Holy Land, the price including accommodation, food, travel and bribes.

The journey could still, however, be difficult and uncomfortable. First pilgrims had to get a licence from their bishop. Everything necessary for the journey had to be taken with them as if going camping – pots and pans, cups, knives, bed linen, and packs of cards and musical instruments to entertain each other. Food could be bought from roadside hawkers who sold fruit, pasties, fish, bread, cakes and wine.

For reasons of safety, pilgrims travelled in groups and were protected by armed guards. Friar Faber set out on a pilgrimage to Jerusalem in 1483 in a party which included six women over eighty years old. Hotel touts would greet the travellers as they approached each town. The hotels were often run by women such as Paula, a Roman who had settled in Bethlehem after making a pilgrimage there. Conditions in the rooms travellers stayed in were often very primitive, even by medieval standards. Instead of having plates, meals were served on thick slices of bread.

The most popular destination for European pilgrims was Santiago de Compostela in Northern Spain, where there was a shrine to St James. This was only a three week round-trip from Britain, including four days at sea in a wooden galley. A trip to the Holy Land could take two years or more, either made overland by walking thirty kilometres a day, or on horseback. Only the wealthier pilgrims, such as the wife of a Norfolk merchant Margery Kempe who set sail for Jerusalem in 1413, could make such long journeys. Many maids, however, did accompany their employers, although because they could not write it is difficult to discover their names and individual stories.

Although pilgrimages were supposed to be undertaken for religious purposes, an added attraction was that they allowed travellers to break free from the customs of their home country. As conditions for travel became more comfortable, complaints arose that the pilgrims were going on their journeys not in search of religious fulfilment but for pleasure. The church authorities became particularly concerned about the large number of women who were undertaking long pilgrimages. They suspected that they might be seeking an opportunity for adventure, and recommendations were made to try and curb their numbers. But women had already established themselves as determined and hardy travellers, prepared to put up with all the discomforts.

*And she had thrice been to Jerusalem;
Had wandered over many a foreign stream;
And she had been at Rome, and at Boulogne,
St James of Compostela, and Cologne;
She knew all about wandering –*
The Wife of Bath, in Geoffrey Chaucer's *Canterbury Tales*, late fourteenth century.

The wealthier pilgrims travelled on horseback. This picture shows a fictional pilgrim, the Wife of Bath, from Chaucer's Canterbury Tales. *It could take a pilgrim up to a year to reach the holy city of Jerusalem.*

Margery Kempe (1373–1438)

The city of Jerusalem.

Margery Kempe was a dedicated pilgrim, going on pilgrimages throughout Britain and to Jerusalem, Rome and Santiago de Compostela in Spain.

Margery Kempe had a comfortable life in England as the wife of a wealthy Norfolk merchant with fourteen children. But she suffered from bouts of depression, and had even once tried to kill herself. She was convinced that she had been saved from death by a vision of Christ, and promised to dedicate her life to him.

She began by visiting all the holy places throughout Britain. Then in 1413, aged forty, she left her family to go on a pilgrimage to Jerusalem which would last two years. She was a woman of strict and unbending principles, which made her unpopular with her more easy-going fellow pilgrims. She would give them lectures on how they should be good Christians, and preach to them about her belief in being a teetotaller and vegetarian.

In Jerusalem, she first experienced what she called 'her cryings' – fits of screaming and convulsions which occurred when she visited religious places. These 'cryings', and her continual complaints at them for drinking wine and eating meat, were too much for the other pilgrims. In revenge, they stole her clothes, cut up her bed sheets, and walked so fast that she could not keep up with them.

But Margery Kempe was a very determined and devout woman, and she put up with these and other hardships in order to complete her pilgrimage. Her enthusiasm was enormous, and when she rode into Jerusalem on the back of a donkey she was so excited that she almost fell off. Afterwards she travelled to Spain and eastern Europe, and made further pilgrimages around England well into her old age.

Margery Kempe's account of her wandering life, *The Book of Margery Kempe*, written in 1436, is the first known travel book in English. But although a woman of wealth and high social status, she was unable to read and write and had to dictate her book. It was not discovered until the 1930s.

2

Grand Tourists

1700–1850

Above *Lady Elizabeth Craven.*

By the end of the sixteenth century most of northern Europe had turned away from the Roman Catholic Church and adopted Protestantism, and pilgrimages were no longer a popular form of travel.

Rather than holy places, wealthy young men were now sent to the fashionable cities of Europe to finish their education. They were expected to study the architecture, visit the art galleries, observe the European way of life and dine with the local nobility. They were supposed to return with a broadened mind,

Below *Illustration of an exotic-looking Turkish couple from an 18th century travel book.*

'

The only use of a gentleman in travelling is to look after the luggage.
Emily Lowe in *Unprotected Females in Norway*, 1857, about her travels with her mother.

'

a good knowledge of foreign languages, and perfect manners. This was considered an excellent training for future diplomats, civil servants and soldiers. Their educational journey, which could last up to three years, became known as the Grand Tour.

Only the upper classes and very wealthy could afford such an extravagance. In 1783 Lady Elizabeth Craven left her husband and six children for a year-long journey to Moscow, St Petersburg, Amsterdam and Vienna. She was a guest at all the fashionable courts, and her high social status meant that she was 'protected by sovereigns and ministers, and treated with respect, and care, and generosity'.

The male Grand Tourists were often teenagers; their average age was eighteen, but many left England at sixteen or younger. Those few women who also travelled were considerably older. Lady Elizabeth Craven had been thirty-five years old when she set out on her journey. While the young male Grand Tourists travelled with a personal tutor to instruct them on the art and history of the countries they visited, the women tourists would often be the wives of diplomats, or would be accompanied by older relatives.

Although the Grand Tourists were very wealthy, travel across Europe could be cramped and uncomfortable. This cartoon makes fun of the conditions of coach travel in Cologne.

'

In the midst of jolts, dust, and weakness from fatigue, the springs of my carriage broke, and threw me into the Ditch. After a considerable delay, we drove on again over such roads or rather rocks, that I felt as if my existence was to snap at every step, and before we could arrive at the next town, the wheel flew off, and again flung me into the middle of the road. Catherine Wilmot, companion to Lord and Lady Mount Cashell on their two-year European tour from 1801-1803. From *An Irish Peer on the Continent (1801-1803). As Related by Catherine Wilmot.*

,

Lady Mary Wortley Montagu (left) wore Turkish dress and visited the closed harems of the Turkish women.

Lady Mary Wortley Montagu went to Constantinople with her husband in 1716 when he was appointed British ambassador to Turkey. The journey took a whole year. The party, with its large following, sailed to Rotterdam, then made an uncomfortable coach ride to Germany and took a boat down the River Danube to Vienna, a popular destination on the Grand Tour. The Viennese court was very lavish, and in winter ladies were taken on horsedrawn sledges over the frozen Danube.

Most of the Grand Tourists were not at all interested in the ordinary people of the countries they visited, but spent their time being entertained in castles and palaces. Some women tourists, however, commented upon the attractive aspects of women's lives in other lands. The veil, they pointed out, had its advantages as a disguise, allowing Turkish women to go about town alone, and undetected by their husbands. Lady Mary Wortley Montagu was particularly curious about the people she travelled amongst, even wearing Turkish dress herself on occasions. She observed how vaccinations were given by the Turkish medicine–women to prevent smallpox, which was then a common and fatal disease. Vaccinations were unknown in Britain at the time, and Lady Mary, after experimenting on her own children, introduced this valuable medical practice to Britain.

The women tourists could go to places that were shut off to men. In 1717, at Sophia in Bulgaria, Lady Mary visited a Turkish bath where the women were bathing, drinking coffee, plaiting each other's hair, and gossiping. 'Such a sight as you never saw in your life and which no book of travellers could inform you of,' she wrote in a letter, because it was 'no less than Death for a Man to be found in one of these places.'

Although their great wealth gave the women Grand Tourists an air of respectability and shielded them from much criticism, their freedom in travelling was still sometimes frowned upon. When Beaujolois Campbell and her mother visited an art gallery in Milan, Italy, they were told by the doorman that there were certain paintings that it was not proper for a young woman to see. 'I was very provoked at him,' wrote Beaujolois, 'Mamma laughed heartily but not to scandalize him we did not ask to see them.'

Many such letters written by the women Grand Tourists were published as books, such as Lady Elizabeth Craven's *A Journey Through the Crimea to Constantinople*, published in 1789. In 1820 Grand Tourist Mariana Starke wrote the first complete travel guide, *Information and Directions for Travellers in the Continent*, which she regularly revised and updated on her trips. Later popular guides, in particular *Murray's* and *Baedeker*, were modelled on Starke's book. The female Grand Tourists had planted women travel writers firmly on the map.

'

Their whole business abroad (as far as I can perceive) being to buy new cloaths, in which they shine in some obscure coffee-house, where they are sure of meeting only one-another . . .
I look upon them as the greatest blockheads.
Lady Mary Wortley Montagu on the Grand Tourists, from *Letters of the Right Honourable Lady Mary Wortley Montagu. Written during her Travels in Europe, Asia and Africa*, 1763.

'

3

Emigrants

1820–1910

The conditions on board ship were often appalling. Many emigrants died on route. This picture shows a ship making for Australia in 1887.

Many people were forced by poverty to travel long distances to find a new and prosperous life. It is difficult to uncover the experiences of the working-class women emigrants, as few recorded what they did and saw. But when organizations were established to help people emigrate, their records can be traced.

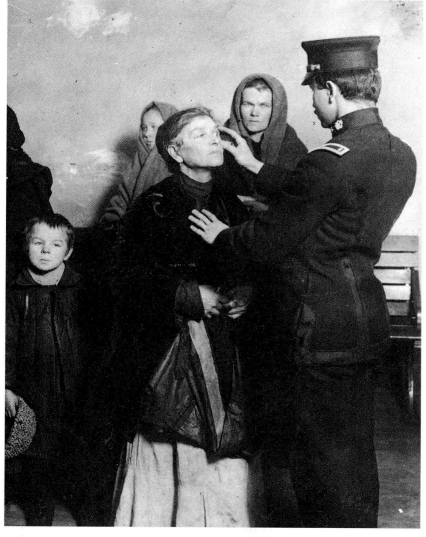

'

God be with you, then, and
speed you, as you cross the
heaving waters,
God be with you, as you land
upon our kinsmen's distant
shore,
Let them feel that Mother
England sends the noblest of
her daughters,
Forges living links of Empire,
links to bind us more and
more.
From 'To England's Daughters'
by Dora Gore Browne in the
Imperial Colonist, December
1904.

'

On arrival in America, women emigrants were given a physical examination.

From the early 1800s, the British Government invested in a number of mass emigration schemes with the hope of solving the problems of poverty in Britain by exporting the poor. The relatively underpopulated continents of North America and Australia, where labourers were in demand and land was available, were the most common destinations. Free or part-paid passages were offered in overcrowded ships. But the emigrants were prepared to put up with appalling conditions in the expectation of wealth in their new homes.

Between 1800 and 1875, seven-and-a-half million people left Britain for Canada alone. Susanna Moodie, who emigrated with her family in 1832, wrote that Canada had become 'the great

'

A settler's wife should be active, industrious, ingenious, cheerful, not above putting her hand to whatever is necessary to be done . . . she must become skilled in the arts of sugar-boiling, candle and soap-making, the making and baking of huge loaves . . . salting meat and fish . . . making clothes for herself, her husband and children; – for there are no tailors.

Catherine Traill, *The Backwoods of Canada Being the Letters from the Wife of an Emigrant Officer,* 1836.

'

landmark for the rich in hope and the poor in purse.' But the new life the emigrants had been promised did not come easily. The winters were colder and the summers were hotter than anything they had experienced before. It was difficult to earn a living from uncultivated land. Rebecca Burlend and her family had been forced through hardship to leave their farm in Yorkshire when the price of corn collapsed, and had sailed to Illinois, North America. When they arrived there was just a piece of uncultivated land for them; they did not even have a cabin to live in and they had to sleep outdoors. It took fourteen years to build up a working, profitable farm.

Some women found that the challenges they faced brought out hidden talents which would have remained undiscovered in Britain. Many of the early settlers showed remarkable determination. In *Life in the Bush*, Mrs Thomson tells how in Australia she learnt to catch and cook a kangaroo, and to bake a parrot pie. Susanna Moodie describes in *Roughing it in the Bush* how she brewed coffee from dandelion roots. There is little, however, about the Maori, Aboriginal or Native American people on whose land they lived in any of their letters home.

By the late 1840s, societies had been established in Britain for the specific purpose of encouraging middle-class female emigrants, such as the Female Middle Class Emigration Society. The 1851 national census revealed a 'surplus' of women over men in the population. *Punch* magazine was worried that there would be a 'petticoat government' and Britain would be 'eaten up by women'. It was feared that women, unable to find a husband, would become redundant and a burden on society. In

A family in pursuit of a homestead, 1886. Once they had arrived in America or Australia, emigrants often had to journey for days or even weeks looking for land on which to build a new home.

America and Australia there were many more white men than white women, so emigration would increase women's chances of getting married. Within three years of its being established in 1849, the Fund for Promoting Female Emigration had sent 1,300 women emigrants abroad. In 1854 the first *Female Emigrant's Guide* was published, written by Catherine Traill who had herself emigrated with her husband to Canada twenty years earlier.

Some middle-class women emigrated as governesses and housekeepers, and found themselves badly treated by their new employers. They had been used to being treated as 'ladies' in Britain, but in their new homes they were regarded as little more than servants. Yet although middle-class Victorian women were often seen as weak and vulnerable, these women's determination and adaptability to their new surroundings show they were not so.

'

Now speed thee, good ship, over sea, and bear us far away,
Where food to eat and friends to greet and work to do await us –
Where without hunger's tempting, we shall not need to pray
Where in wedlock's tie, not harlotry, we shall find men to mate us.
'Needlewoman's Farewell', *Punch*, January 1850.

'

Many single women went abroad as nannies. This photograph shows a nanny with children in North America in 1912.

The Aboriginal people lived in Australia long before the emigrants from Europe arrived. But in the emigrants' accounts of their new lands, the local people are seldom mentioned.

By the beginning of the twentieth century, the African continent had been fought over and seized by the European powers. It was partitioned into forty political units, thirty-six of which were controlled by either Britain, France or Germany. European powers were also busy establishing colonies in Asia. In Britain, women were told it was their 'imperial duty' to get married and have sons in the colonies in order to populate them with a ruling, white race. Between 1901–10, 4,000 single women went to Cape Colony (part of present-day South Africa) assisted by the emigration societies.

It is important to remember that while travel and emigration might have provided opportunities for a better life for British women, it was often to the disadvantage of those they would be living amongst.

4

Missionaries and Nurses

1850–1920

By the mid-nineteenth century, British missionary societies were expanding into Asia and Africa. During the early days of missionary work, the only British women who went abroad were wives sent out with their husbands to the mission stations. Anna Hinderer went to Abeokuta in south-western Nigeria in 1852 as 'mother, playfellow, teacher' to her 'flock'. The famous African missionary David Livingstone's father-in-law thought that, 'A missionary without a wife . . . is like a boat with only one oar. A good missionary's wife can be as useful as her husband in the Lord's vineyard.'

A missionary wife's role was to complement the work of her husband, looking after the needs of the local women and children. This missionary couple were stationed in India in 1898.

‘

It is to women Missionaries that we must look as the most efficient instruments for dealing with women and children – in getting at their hearts and minds, and in seeking to raise them to a higher level of purity. From Bishop Alfred R. Tucker, *Eighteen Years in Uganda and East Africa*, 1908.

’

The missionary authorities grew concerned about the high death rate among missionary wives, mostly caused by the strain of giving birth and raising their children in quite simple living conditions. The missionary societies therefore established special 'Ladies Committees' to recruit single women. By 1900, 8,000 women missionaries were employed throughout the world, almost half of the total number of missionaries.

Like the wives, the single women missionaries were thought to have a special role. In India and Muslim regions they could enter the private quarters of a house and talk to the women as no male missionary could. The women missionaries were put in charge of the needs of the women and children, such as education and health.

The women missionaries were also supposed, by example and teaching, to train African and Asian women to be 'good Christian wives'. They gave them lessons in knitting, needlework and how to lay a table correctly. The qualities looked for in a female missionary candidate were not toughness and an ability to adapt to her surroundings, as had been needed for the women emigrants. Instead the missionary societies looked for piety, neatness, a quiet voice and a submissive manner.

In practice, however, many women applied to be missionaries because they wanted to go 'into the bush' and be physically and mentally challenged at a remote missionary station. Behind the disguise of doing a job acceptable for a woman, missionary work provided an escape from the pressure to marry and the boredom of being a stay-at-home spinster. Christina Forsyth left the West Coast of Scotland in 1878 for south-eastern Africa and soon asked to work away from any other Europeans. She remained at her remote mission station in Fingoland for thirty years. In Britain she earned the nickname 'the loneliest woman in Africa', although she was by no means alone, surrounded by African neighbours and friends.

Many of the missionary women became legends in their own lifetime and were celebrated as heroines on their return to Britain. They lectured on their travels throughout the country, raising money for missionary work. Many popular books were written about them – among them *Heroines of the Cross, Women of Worth*, and *Women in the Mission Field* – as examples to young women to take up God's calling and follow in their footsteps.

From the late 1880s onwards, many women missionaries went on a brief medical training course before leaving Britain. They learnt how to cope with tropical diseases and midwifery. The missionary societies did not recognize any value in traditional African and Asian treatments, and sought to introduce

'
I have seen her go down under fire with her little store of creature comforts for our wounded men, and a more tender or skilful hand about a wound or a broken limb could not be found amongst our best surgeons.
William Russell, war correspondent for *The Times*, writing about Mary Seacole, c.1855.
,

Western medical practices, especially for childbirth. The women missionaries were thought to be particularly suited to this. Societies were set up in Britain to raise funds for this area of their work, such as the National Association for Supplying Female Medical Aid to the Women of India, which was established in 1885.

Women missionaries were given particular responsibility for looking after local children, often setting up schools and providing basic medical care.

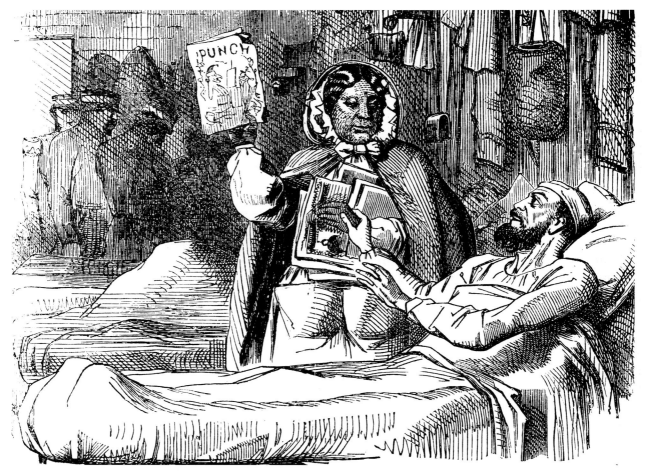

Mary Seacole tended to British troops during the Crimean War. Many knew her as the black Florence Nightingale.

Nurses who were not missionaries also went to look after British soldiers, emigrants and colonial employees abroad. Many were encouraged by Florence Nightingale and Mary Seacole, who had both nursed in the Crimean War (in what is present-day Soviet Union), in the 1850s. Mary Seacole, a black 'doctress' from Jamaica whose services had been refused by Florence Nightingale's nursing association, wrote an account of her amazing life called *Wonderful Adventures of Mrs Seacole in Many Lands.*

In 1897, the Colonial Nursing Association (CNA) was formed to employ nurses for the growing British colonial communities in Africa and Asia. Within the first five years, the CNA sent over a hundred paid nurses to clinics and hospitals around the world. By the time the Boer War broke out in South Africa at the turn of the century, nurses were seen as such a vital part of caring for white men abroad that thousands were sent out from Britain to treat the soldiers and prisoners of war.

Mary Slessor (1848–1915)

Mary Slessor was a pioneer missionary who rose from a working-class background in Dundee, Scotland, to become one of the most famous women in Britain.

Her father was an alcoholic, and when he lost his job in 1859 eleven-year-old Mary was forced to become a weaver to provide her family with an income. She received some education at night school, but was largely self-taught.

Mary became involved with the local United Presbyterian Church, working as a voluntary teacher and supporting missionary work. The publicity surrounding the death of the famous missionary David Livingstone in 1873 was an inspiration to her, as it was to many others, and she applied to the Church to work abroad. At the age of twenty-seven she was at last accepted by the Foreign Mission Board as a teacher in Calabar, Nigeria. In August 1876 she sailed for West Africa, having never left Scotland before.

Mary Slessor quickly picked up the local Efik language and immersed herself in work amongst the women. She was soon applying for a remote station where she could live more cheaply and send more of her annual salary to her family in Scotland. The missionary society allowed her to move just five kilometres inland. But this was only the first step in a gradual journey away from European settlement on the coast.

When her mother and sister both died in 1886, Mary's last links with home were broken. Moving still further inland, she dispensed with the trappings of the colonial lifestyle – drank unboiled water, used no mosquito net, walked barefoot and even

went without a hat, which was considered scandalous. Visitors commented upon the tiny Scotswoman's sunburnt face and unkempt appearance. When the traveller Mary Kingsley visited her in 1895, she found Mary Slessor 'has lost most of her missionary ideas and bullies the native chiefs in their own tongue . . . and is regarded by the other missionaries as mad and dangerous.'

In 1892 she was appointed Vice-Consul in Okoyong, judging over the Native Court. Mary Slessor was a natural meddler with an iron will, so the role of magistrate suited her well. She was continuously petitioning the district officer concerning injustices, particularly on behalf of the women. It is said that no woman lost a case while Miss Slessor was in the chair.

By 1907 arthritis had almost crippled her, but she refused to move either to the comfort of Duke Town or return to Britain. She died on 13 January 1915 and was buried in Calabar.

Above *Isabella Bird made a living by lecturing and writing books about her worldwide travels.*

Below *Unlike women travellers, male explorers, such as Henry Morton Stanley, often employed hundreds of porters to carry their equipment.*

5

Lady Explorers

1870–1910

European countries continued to conquer and occupy large parts of Africa and Asia in the late nineteenth century, in order to subject the local people to colonial rule. At the forefront of the imperial endeavour were the male explorers, who mapped out areas previously unknown to Europeans so they could be more easily administered and controlled.

Many of these explorers were backed by government grants, newspapers or immense personal wealth. They could employ vast numbers of porters, guides and interpreters, and travel thousands of kilometres. Henry Morton Stanley, with money from the *Daily Telegraph*, took three years to cross the continent of Africa from 1874–77. As did most male explorers, he took an enormous amount of equipment with him, weighing eight

tonnes, including two crates of photographic equipment, shaving mirrors, ivory-backed hairbrushes and eau de cologne. He employed three hundred porters to carry the loads.

At the same time, the ideal of Victorian womanhood demanded that middle-class women remain behind as the 'Angel in the Home'. For many women, however, the appeal of distant lands full of lush jungles, snow-capped mountains and rushing rapids was far more attractive than any role offered them within their own society. They were prepared to take enormous personal risks and face much discomfort in order to, above all else, live a little.

For women who had sat quiet and unnoticed in the corner of a stuffy Victorian parlour, looking after sick relatives, doing embroidery, and attending tea parties, the new freedom they found abroad was intoxicating. 'You feel the bands break that were riveted about your heart,' wrote Gertrude Bell from the Middle East in 1905, a region whose language, history and culture had captivated her, and where she would soon make her home. Forty-year-old Marianne North left Britain in 1871 when her father died, and spent the next fifteen years travelling around the world making remarkable, colourful paintings of the luscious tropical plants she saw. Isabella Bird revelled in

'
I am well as long as I live on horseback . . . sleep out-of-doors, or in a log cabin, and lead in all respects a completely unconventional life. But each time for a few days . . . I have become civilised, I have found myself rapidly going down again.
Isabella Bird Bishop in *A Lady's Life in the Rocky Mountains*, 1879.
'

Below *Ella Christie, who left Scotland in 1902 for a life of travel. She boasted that she had visited every country in Europe, as well as China, Japan, Central Asia and a trip on the trans-Siberian railway.* **Below left** *A picture taken by Ella Christie of some Burmese children. To the people they travelled amongst, women explorers were strange objects of wonder and suspicion.*

'*The Rajah lent me a cook, a soldier, and a boy, gave me a lot of bread, a coopful of chickens, and packed us all into a canoe, in which we pulled through small canals and forest nearly all day; then landed at a village, and walked up 700 feet of beautiful zigzag road, to the clearing in the forest . . . Life was very delicious up there.* Marianne North in Sarawak in 1876, from *Recollections of a Happy Life*, 1892.*'*

Marianne North's ambition was to paint as many tropical plants as possible in their natural home. She made over a thousand oil paintings of specimens in India, Borneo, South Africa, Jamaica and the Seychelles.

there being, 'No door bells, no "please mems", no dirt, no bills, no demands of any kind,' when she set out on her world-wide travels. The middle-aged spinster said at last she felt like a girl of twenty-one. The illness that had plagued her at home in Edinburgh disappeared the moment she was out in the open and on horseback in a distant country.

The Victorian lady explorers did not have the financial backing enjoyed by male travellers, so they could employ only a handful of guides and travelled with less luggage. But they did take with them many of the same attitudes as the men. In particular, they believed that they were racially superior to the black peoples amongst whom they travelled. It was this superiority which, they believed, would protect them from any danger. Their white skins and wealth made them very visible, and also implied to the local people that they were members of a conquering, colonial power.

Back in Britain, however, the sex of the explorer mattered very much indeed. The women explorers came under attack in the newspapers for acting outside their proper role. After

A map showing the routes through China and Japan taken by Mary Gaunt, Ella Christie and Isabella Bird.

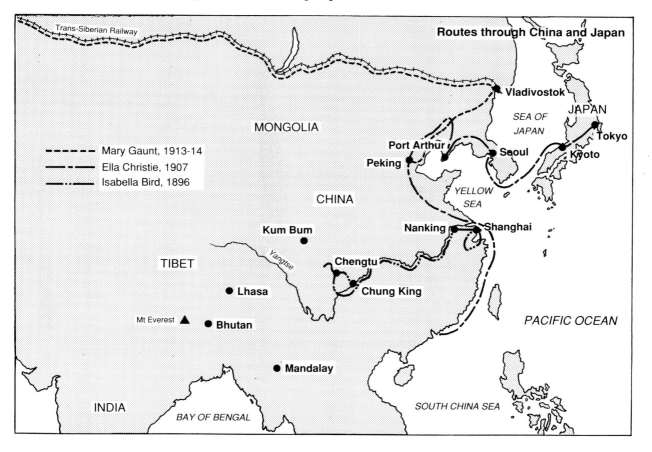

several long debates, the influential Royal Geographical Society refused to admit them as members. In response to this criticism of them, the women explorers emphasized how they had acted very properly while on their travels. When *The Times* reported that Isabella Bird had worn male clothes while riding for 'greater convenience', she was furious and wrote back immediately. She explained that her riding costume was an 'American Lady's Mountain Dress', 'a thoroughly serviceable and feminine costume'. In Britain, many of the women travellers were forced in public to deny the very freedom and independence which, in private, they so desperately sought.

This map shows the routes through Africa taken by Mary Kingsley, Mary Gaunt and Marianne North.

Routes through Africa

'
——————————

A lady explorer? a traveller in skirts?
The notion's just a trifle too seraphic:
Let them stay and mind the babies, or hem our ragged shirts;
But they musn't, can't, and shan't be geographic.
Punch, 1893.

'

——— – Mary Kingsley, 1893 and 1895
– – – – – Mary Gaunt, 1908 and 1910
•••••• Marianne North, 1882-83

Mary Kingsley (1862–1900)

Imagine a typical Victorian spinster, and you imagine Mary Kingsley. In her stiff black dress, high-necked blouse, and carrying a big black umbrella, she looked as if she had never ventured further than her London home. But this slight young woman had, by 1896, made two extraordinary journeys along the rivers and through the rainforests of West Africa.

After years of living at home caring for her sick mother, in 1892 Mary Kingsley found herself suddenly set free when both her parents died within a couple of months of each other. She was thirty, and she felt she had to do something with her life at last, before it was too late. She decided to sail for West Africa, taking with her jars of spirits to preserve specimens of plants and insects.

West Africa in the 1890s was known as the 'White Man's Grave'. The high death rate amongst Europeans, caused by tropical diseases and in particular malaria, made the region an unattractive area. But Mary Kingsley wanted to get as far as possible from the comforts and restraints of her home life.

She made two journeys to Africa. The first, in 1893, lasted only six months, and she kept quite close to the coast. On her second year-long journey in 1895, she hired two canoes and nine guides, and went upriver into the interior of Gabon, rushing over rapids, sleeping in the open air, and bathing in the tropical streams. She felt exhilarated.

On her return to Britain, Mary felt honour-bound to defend the Africans who had looked after her on her journey. The missionary societies looked upon them as children who should be educated to European ways, but Mary wanted West African lifestyles to be preserved. She defended polygamy, which allowed one man to take many wives, as appropriate to the West African way of life. Everything had to be looked at from the African's point of view, she said, and then it made sense. She called it sympathy for the black man, 'not emotional but common sense sympathy and honour and appreciation.'

Her first book, *Travels in West Africa*, published in 1897, was an immediate bestseller. Her controversial views gave her a wide audience. However, the demands on her time in Britain to give lectures and write articles for the newspapers prevented her from returning to Africa. When there was a demand for nurses as a result of the Boer War in South Africa in early 1900, she saw an opportunity to leave and applied.

The conditions in which she worked in the makeshift hospital in South Africa were appalling, and within two months she had caught the same typhoid fever that was killing her patients. Mary Kingsley died on 3 June 1900.

6

Anthropologists

1910 Onwards

Anthropology, the study of people and the way they live, developed as a science after the turn of the century, when universities began to offer anthropology courses and fieldwork was beginning to be recognized as a necessary part of anthropological research. Before this time, 'armchair anthropologists' used to gather material from travellers' tales and construct general theories from them, without ever having travelled to the countries or met the people they were writing about.

Right *Audrey Richards. Her research in East Africa was amongst the earliest work on how foreign societies lived.*
Above *Margaret Mead, an American anthropologist, was a founder of modern anthropological methods.*

As anthropology was a new profession there were fewer qualifications needed to take it up, so women, with less access to educational opportunities, were able to contribute as field-workers and writers. Unlike the Royal Geographical Society, the Anthropological Institute had admitted women as members since the 1870s. By the 1920s, while other sciences were still closed to them, women were already getting a name for their anthropological work. In 1928, the American anthropologist Margaret Mead published her famous *Coming of Age in Samoa*, written about the fieldwork she had done in the Pacific. Its descriptions of the relationship between men and women on the island make this one of the most pioneering books on anthropology ever published.

The Royal Geographical Society did not admit women until 1913, although they could attend meetings as the guest of a male member.

Top and bottom *At the end of the 19th century Daisy Bates left Ireland to go to Australia. For more than fifty years she lived there, studying the Aboriginal way of life.*

As with missionary work, it was soon realized that women could make a particular contribution to anthropological field-work through their special contact with foreign women. Men mostly wrote about political organizations and public life, while the female anthropologists concentrated on what went on inside African and Asian homes. Mrs Amaury Talbot and her husband were assigned a special area of study: while he wrote more general studies, she began writing with 'no intervening male influence' of the 'women's mysteries' in West Africa, 'information denied [her husband] by ancient law'. Her research produced one of the earliest anthropological works on West African women, *Women's Mysteries of a Primitive People*, published in 1915.

Other women were attracted to fieldwork by the opportunity it gave to live away from major towns and European popula-tions. Daisy Bates left Ireland at the end of the nineteenth cen-tury to visit friends in Australia. Fifty years later she was still there, living in a tent and recording the Aboriginal lifestyle that was already under threat. She described the ceremonies around conception, birth, puberty, marriage and death, and translated legends and songs. She wrote one of the first major works on the Aboriginal people and became 'an authority on all things aboriginal'.

Daisy Bates claimed, like many women anthropologists, to be particularly sensitive to the feelings of so-called 'primitive' peoples. She said that she thought with a 'black man's mind'. Women anthropologists were in the forefront of those who argued that foreign societies must be examined from their own point of view. Only then could they be fully understood.

Daisy Bates, like women anthropologists who followed her, was accused of being sentimental about her subject of study. Close contact with the local peoples, living in their villages and adopting their way of life, was disapproved of. Daisy Bates was called with disgust, 'the woman who lives with the blacks'. Women's reports were often treated with suspicion, because it was thought that they were less impartial than men.

While some women anthropologists argued for academic detachment in all they wrote and saw, others wanted to include their own personal impressions. So far away from home, and often in such extraordinary surroundings, it was impossible to be cold and distant about their experiences. When a well known American anthropologist wanted to publish an account of her fieldwork among the Tiv people in West Africa which included her own feelings, she felt unable to do so. She was anxious that it might destroy her scientific reputation. Instead she

'

It is the fashion among journalists and others to talk of the 'lawless Albanians'. But there is perhaps no other people in Europe so much under the tyranny of laws . . . And lest you that read this book should cry out the 'customs of savages', I would remind you that we play the game on a much larger scale and call it war.
Edith Durham, *High Albania*, 1909.

'

published under a false name, and said the book was a novel, although it was based on her true experiences. The name she used was Elenore Smith Bowen, and the novel was called *Return to Laughter*, published in 1954. This debate about women travellers' ability to report with scientific objectivity on the places they visit continues to this day.

> *By the wells and the creeks, sitting in the camps in the firelight, on horse-back and on foot my notebook and pencil were always with me. I would come out sometimes for days, sharing my food, nursing the babies, gathering vegetable food with the women . . . until I gained a unique insight into the whole northern aboriginal social system . . . Every moment of my spare time was given to this self-imposed and fascinating study.*
>
> Daisy Bates, *The Passing of the Aborigines*, 1938.

Mary Leakey, anthropologist, at work with her husband in Tanganyika.

Audrey Isabel Richards (1899–1984)

The work of Dr Audrey Richards shaped the development of anthropology in its most crucial early years.

Audrey Richards came from an educated middle-class family, so it was not all that surprising when, aged twenty-three, she took a degree at Cambridge University. What was surprising, however, was that she studied science; very few women did so in the early 1920s. And even more unusual was for her to take this scientific training and apply it to one of the new areas of research – anthropology.

For the next ten years, Audrey Richards carried out her fieldwork in East Africa, and Zambia in particular. It was the daily details of people's lives that interested her. She was soon making more trips to study marriage, fertility and eating habits – areas that other anthropologists ignored. Her first book, *Hunger and Work in a Savage Tribe*, was published in 1932.

Dr Audrey Richards.

Dr Richards thought it was her duty as a scholar to make the information she gathered as widely available as possible, especially to the people whom she had studied. When she did fieldwork in an East African village, in return she collected stories of their ancestors and printed them for the villagers. But she also thought it important that her research was used by the British Colonial Office to help people to understand the changes colonialism had brought to African peoples.

Although she lectured often and held many posts in universities, she did not fit easily into the male-dominated academic establishment. 'I have never run a "school"

or been a professor,' she boasted, proud of her independence. But in recognition of her work, in 1959 she was made the President of the Royal Anthropological Institute – the only woman ever to have held that post.

Dr Richards would never have called herself a feminist. But she did much to promote women in anthropology by her example. She also focused on African women in her fieldwork. *Chisungu*, published in 1956, about the rituals of Bemba girls growing up in Zambia, is considered her most important book.

When she retired in 1967, Dr Richards had been active in anthropology for half a century.

7

Holidaymakers

1950 Onwards

After the Second World War times were tough, and people were longing to get away from dreary Britain for sun and fun.

Travel agent Thomas Cook had been conducting all-in tours since the 1840s, but it had mainly been the wealthy and the determined who had travelled abroad. With the introduction of compulsory paid holidays in the 1930s, cheap mass travel for working-class people began to develop on a larger scale. In 1952 the first jet passenger plane, the Comet, came into service and holidays by air were offered. Until this time, air travel had been reserved for the rich and adventurous. Air stewardesses were now introduced on flights. Because so many passengers were sick, the first stewardesses were required to be registered nurses and wear nurses' uniforms.

In October 1958, the Comet offered the first transatlantic passenger service.

Two young women getting ready for a cycling holiday, in the early 1950s. The number of women travelling alone or with other women was on the increase.

Package holidays allowed many British families to go abroad for the first time. The benefits of tourism were considered so great that the United Nations declared 1967 International Year of the Tourist. A resolution was passed recognizing tourism as 'a basic and most desirable human activity, deserving the praise and encouragement of all peoples and all governments.' By the 1980s, tourism was the largest and fastest-growing industry in the world. In 1988, twenty million British people went abroad on holiday.

For women with children, and older people, a package holiday can offer greater comfort, less worries, and is generally a safe way to travel. Women on package holidays are not in general looking for new experiences and challenges, but a chance to relax away from work and home. Yet sticking to areas where there are many tourists is not always as straightforward as it may seem. In all countries, there are ways in which women are expected to behave, and without realizing it a female tourist can offend these. How a woman dresses is often considered particularly important. A woman on holiday may see nothing wrong in wearing shorts and a T-shirt. But in many Muslim countries, it is considered improper to show your arms, legs and hair. In the Pacific Islands, however, it is thought more daring to expose your ankles than your breasts. If women tourists ignore these customs, they may be seen as acting improperly and as 'available for sex'.

There are other problems concerned with mass tourism which affect both male and female tourists, and the countries

'

When the tourists flew in
our men put aside
their fishing nets
to become waiters –
our women became whores

When the tourists flew in
what culture we had flew out
of the window –
we traded our customs
for sunglasses and pop –
From a poem by Cecil Rajendra, a Malaysian protest poet.

'

With the introduction of cheap rail passes for young people, such as Interrail in the early 1980s, young women with rucksacks travelling independently became a common sight in Europe.

'————

As for tourists how do Moroccans see them? If a woman is alone or only with women, what kind of woman can she be? No father would put his daughter at risk by letting her travel unless she was already 'worthless' . . . She sits in cafes, drinks alcohol, smokes cigarettes . . . and will even comb her hair in public. She often dresses 'indecently' – not even a prostitute would do this. Pat Chell, 'Three Kinds of Women', in *Women Travel. Adventures, Advice and Experience*, 1990.

————'

which they travel to. Environmental issues have become a particular cause for concern. Polluted beaches, the erosion of mountain paths, and even traffic jams are just some of them. In Egypt, for example, the large number of people climbing the ancient pyramids may have damaged the stones.

Mass tourism can also harm a country's culture. Local architecture may be replaced by high-rise hotels to accommodate more guests, and local restaurants may start to serve the tourists the same food they would eat at home. Those expressions of local culture which are to be seen are often fake and are put on for tourists who want exotic, 'native' experiences, but without taking any risks. Shows may be staged where the local people dress up in their 'traditional' costumes and are photographed. Much of this dress and dance is in fact invented for foreign visitors. For example, a belly-dancing display may be offered on package holidays to an Arab country where in fact it was never practised.

One result of mass tourism which particularly affects local women are the 'sex tours' offered in some Far East holiday destinations. Patpong, a district of Thailand's capital Bangkok, is known throughout the world for its go-go bars and brothels which cater for Western male tourists and businessmen. More than three million tourists visit Thailand each year, and almost 70 per cent of these tourists are male. There are an estimated 700,000 prostitutes working in Thailand, mostly aged between seventeen and twenty-four. Many Thai girls come from the poor countryside to the cities and resorts where, as a prostitute, they can earn ten times the wage of a waitress and send money back to their families.

8

Adventurers

1970 Onwards

Following the demands of the women's liberation movement in the 1960s, women began to take part in many areas of life from which they had previously been excluded. The argument that women were too physically weak for activities that put heavy demands on their bodies had at last been challenged. Opportunities opened up for women mountaineers, sailors and sportswomen of all kinds.

In September 1977, Naomi James, a hairdresser with just six weeks' yachting experience, set sail from Dartmouth on the south coast of England. She became the first woman to sail solo around the world. Like many women who have achieved remarkable records of physical and mental endurance, Naomi James insisted that she did not set out to prove that women could do as well as men. 'I wasn't interested in proving anything to anyone except myself,' she said.

Julie Tullis was the first woman to join the British Everest Expedition in 1985, and the first woman in the world to climb over 8,000 metres. She had a favourite Himalayan mountain, known as K2, and it was her lifelong desire to climb it. She reached the summit on 5 August 1986, but her triumph was brief. Within a few days, she was killed in a snow storm. She had written in her autobiography, 'If I could choose a place to die it would be in the mountains.'

As were the female Grand Tourists over two hundred years ago, today's women adventurers are often older than the men who make similar courageous journeys. Julie Tullis did not start her mountaineering career until she was thirty-eight years old. Like many women travellers, she did not want to leave her children for long periods before they were old enough to look after themselves. Bicyclist Bettina Selby waited until she was forty-seven before pedalling across the Himalayas. Since then, she has taken her bike across Europe and the Middle East, along the length of the River Nile and through the Saharan desert to Timbuktu. She enjoys the discomforts, she says, which are such a contrast to her cosy life at home in a London suburb.

Kriter Lady II, *the boat on which Naomi James sailed solo around the world in 1978.*

'

When a man sees you struggle with a rope on deck, he immediately comes to take it off you. He doesn't let you do it for yourself. He thinks you're incapable. Another woman lets you get on with it, and that way you learn.
Tracy Edwards.

'

'
The challenge is to myself and not the mountain.
Julie Tullis, *Clouds from Both Sides*, 1986.
'

Above *Julie Tullis was Britain's foremost female mountaineer. The picture on the right shows her at the top of Lost Arrow in Yosemite, USA.*

In 1989 Helen Sharman heard a news flash on her car radio – 'Astronaut Wanted – No Experience Necessary' – and jotted down the phone number. Competing with 13,000 other applicants, in March 1991 she was chosen to join a Soviet mission to the space station *Mir*. She was the first British person to go up in space.

Many women adventurers travel entirely on their own and have little contact with other women travellers. But some women adventurers choose to travel with other women, forming all-female expeditions. In 1990, twelve women took part in the round-the-world yacht race. They became the first all-female crew to round treacherous Cape Horn. In 1978, a team of American women attempted to climb Annapurna I in the Himalayas. At 8,000 m it is the tenth highest mountain in the world. The leader, Dr Arlene Blum, had been rejected for another climbing expedition on the grounds of her sex. In defiance, the Annapurna women all wore T-shirts with the slogan 'A Woman's Place is on Top – of Annapurna' printed on them.

> *The trip was easy . . . The two important things that I did learn were that you are as powerful and strong as you allow yourself to be, and that the most difficult part of any endeavour is taking the first step.*
> Robyn Davidson, *Tracks*, 1980. Robyn Davidson trekked 2,700 km across the Australian desert, with just her camels for company.

A map showing the route of the Whitbread round-the-world yacht race.

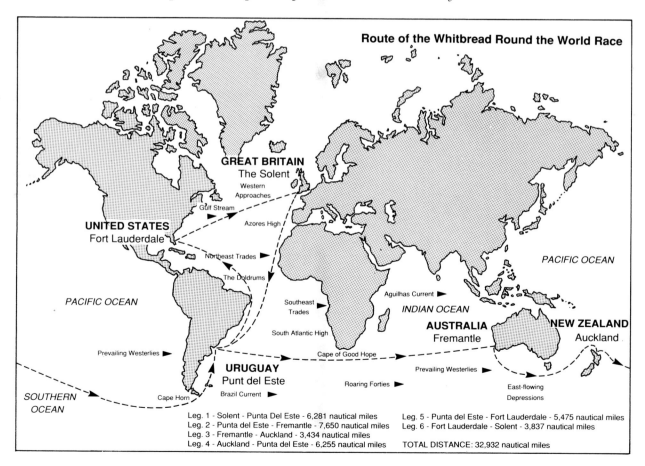

Route of the Whitbread Round the World Race

Leg. 1 - Solent - Punta Del Este - 6,281 nautical miles
Leg. 2 - Punta del Este - Fremantle - 7,650 nautical miles
Leg. 3 - Fremantle - Auckland - 3,434 nautical miles
Leg. 4 - Auckland - Punta del Este - 6,255 nautical miles
Leg. 5 - Punta del Este - Fort Lauderdale - 5,475 nautical miles
Leg. 6 - Fort Lauderdale - Solent - 3,837 nautical miles

TOTAL DISTANCE: 32,932 nautical miles

Tracy Edwards (born 1962)

On 28 May 1990, after sailing 53,000 km across the world's oceans, Tracy Edwards skippered the yacht *Maiden* into Southampton. It was the first time an all-female crewed vessel had completed the Whitbread round-the-world race, the most difficult yacht race ever run. 'Home are the Heroines' blasted the newspaper headlines. Tracy Edwards was more modest. 'They said it was impossible. They told us we couldn't do it. But we did it,' she said.

It was while sailing in an earlier race as a cook, the only way a woman could take part, that Tracy had the idea of an all-female race entry. She sold her house to raise the money, and began to assemble a crew. Over 400 women applied to join her boat. She had plenty of enthusiasm, but finding enough money to equip the yacht was more difficult. Tracy was not looking for luxury. Far less money was needed than for any of the all-male boats entering the Whitbread race, yet over 300 companies refused Tracy's appeals for sponsorship. Finally Royal Jordanian Airlines came forward and offered her help.

The women she picked for her crew had to be tough. They worked watches of four hours on, four hours off, around the clock. They never got more than three and a half hours sleep at one time. As they crossed the Equator, the temperature soared and the deck was too hot to walk on without thick soles. Sailing through the Southern Ocean, it became so cold their cheeks were frostbitten. For nine months, with stormforce winds, torn sails, spinal injuries and a leak which flooded over their bunks, the twelve women sailors battled with the elements. No one believed they would be able to complete the race; many thought they would die in the attempt.

But they not only completed the race, they came first in their division in two of the six legs. Twenty-seven-year-old Tracy Edwards became the first woman to receive the Yachtsman(!) of the Year Award.

Tracy Edwards, skipper of the first all-female crew in the round-the-world race.

9

Women Travellers Today

Women travellers used to be isolated individuals who rarely met each other. Today, more and more groups and clubs are being formed to bring together women who travel to discuss their particular problems and experiences. The Business Women's Travel Club was founded in 1987 to discuss the particular needs of women who have to go abroad for their work. In the USA, the Society of Women Geographers has regular meetings throughout the country so women can discuss the study they have undertaken abroad. In Britain, the Royal Geographical Society held its first 'Women and Travel' day in March 1991.

In the 1990s, many women now travel the world on business.

English nurse, Susie Wighton (on the far left), helping to hand out food in a Palestinian refugee camp in Beirut.

Publishers are beginning to reprint books written by earlier women travellers, including the early pilgrims and Victorian lady explorers. These show that women have always been on the move. As women today learn that many others have travelled before them, it gives them courage to take that first step on the path themselves.

But there are many differences between travellers today and those of the past. Many modern travellers see the need to take account of conditions in the country through which they travel and show respect for cultures different from their own. Scottish art student Susie Wighton felt that simply going on a journey through the Middle East was not enough. 'I decided I couldn't do much for the world painting pictures,' she said, 'So I thought I would train as a nurse. I wanted to change things not just travel.' She was thrust to fame in 1986 when the Palestinian refugee camp in Beirut in which she worked was besieged.

Many travellers are increasingly aware of having to give back something to those foreign countries and people who have treated them so kindly. Deborah Rutter in Nepal remembers how the Nepalese women invited her into their kitchens and gave her food. She wrote, 'They would wave aside any thanks and say, "if we came as strangers to your country, you would feed us, wouldn't you?"'

Projects

1 Keeping a travel diary:

Next time you go away – to stay with friends or relatives, sightseeing, to the seaside, on holiday – keep a diary of what you see. If you are going with a friend, brother or sister, ask them to keep a diary too.

When you get home, read through your diary. As you are reading, think of the following questions and keep the answers on a separate piece of paper.

• What did you record? Why did you record these things instead of others? Did you write down, for example, what you ate? Did you write down what kind of buildings you saw?

• If something was very strange and different from your life at home, did that make you write it down?

• Did you write anything about the people you stayed with or saw? Did you, for example, write down how people were dressed?

• Did you write down how you felt about being away from home? Did it make you feel different? Did you act differently?

If your friend, brother or sister kept a travel diary too, are there any big differences between your diary and theirs? Did you notice different things? If so, why do you think this was? If you were a different sex, do you think you would have noticed and written down different things?

2 Older women's travels:

Find out what journeys older women in your family or neighbourhood – perhaps your grandmother, aunt or a next-door neighbour – made when they were younger. They may have had to move to work, to visit friends or family far away, or just gone on holiday. You may be surprised to discover how many older women have travelled.

Using a tape recorder, talk to an older woman who has made a journey. Make a list of questions you would like to ask her. Here are some ideas:

• Where did you go, and for how long?

• Why did you go?

• Were you enthusiastic about going, or did you want to stay at home?

• Did you travel alone or in a group? Were there any other women travelling with you?

• Who did you talk to and make friends with on your travels? Did you make more friends with women or with men? Why do you think this was?

• What sort of problems did you have travelling? Were there specific problems because you were a woman?

• Have you travelled since? Do you notice differences between when you first travelled many years ago and travelling today?

3 Travels in the past:

Try to imagine you have never left the neighbourhood in which you live. Then suddenly you go very far away – somewhere in Africa, say. How do you think you would react? Would you be scared? What would you miss? Would you try to adapt to the new country you were in, or would you hold on to what you were used to at home? For example, would you dress like you do now or would you dress like the locals?

Look at chapters one to five. All the women in these chapters made just such journeys far away from everything that was familiar to them. Compare their reactions to how you imagined you would react. What does this make you think of these earlier women?

Books to Read

Books for younger readers

Barr, Pat *A Curious Life for a Lady. The Story of Isabella Bird* (Secker and Warburg, 1970)

Birkett, Dea 'Mary Kingsley and West Africa' in Marsden, Gordon (ed.) *Victorian Values Personalities and Perspectives in Nineteenth Century Society* (Longman, 1990)

Blanch, Lesley *The Wilder Shores of Love* (John Murray, 1989)

Davies, Miranda and others (eds.) *Half the Earth Women's Experiences of Travel World-wide* (Pandora, 1986)

Davies, Miranda and Jansz, Natania (eds.) *Women Travel. Adventures, Advice and Experience* (Harrap, 1990)

Edwards, Tracy and Madge, Tim *Maiden* (Simon and Schuster, 1990)

Grosskurth, Phyllis *Margaret Mead A Life of Controversy* (Penguin, 1988)

Middleton, Dorothy *Victorian Lady Travellers*, (Antique Collectors Club, 1965)

Russell, Mary *The Blessings of a Good Thick Skirt Women Travellers and Their World* (Collins, 1986)

Books for older readers

Allcock, John and Young, Antonia (eds.) *Black Lambs and Grey Falcons Women Travellers in the Balkans* (Bradford University Press, 1991)

Birkett, Dea *Spinsters Abroad Victorian Lady Explorers* (Blackwell, 1989)

Robinson, Jane *Wayward Women* (Oxford University Press, 1990)

Glossary

Aborigines The first inhabitants of Australia, who lived there before the white people arrived. They are now severely reduced in number.

Anthropology The study of how people live and organize their lives, such as their family relationships, religion and laws.

Autobiography The story of one's own life, written by oneself.

Colonization The control and government by force of one country or people by a group of foreigners, usually referring to former European control of parts of Africa and Asia.

Diplomat A person who goes abroad as a representative of their government, to meet and talk to foreign government officials.

Economic Concerned with income and finance.

Emigrants People who leave their home and country to live and work abroad.

Fieldwork Studies undertaken on the spot, such as going to a faraway village to talk to the people about their lives, or collecting botanical specimens.

Governess A woman teacher employed in a private home to educate the children.

Grand Tour A journey around Europe by young aristocratic British people in the eighteenth and early nineteenth centuries. It was intended to complete their education.

Harlotry Prostitution.

Impartial Without preferences or prejudices.

Interpreters People who translate the spoken word from one language to another.

Medieval A period of history from approximately AD 500–1450.

Midwifery The practice and skill of helping a woman to give birth.

Mission station The missionary's home, together with other buildings such as a school and church, which make up the missionary's headquarters abroad.

Missionary A person sent by the Church to preach, teach and work in a foreign country.

Muslim Of the religion of Islam.

Objectivity A position of looking at something with detachment, without allowing personal feelings and opinions to colour your judgement.

Penance Voluntary self-punishment to atone for a sin.

Piety Devotion to religious duties.

Pilgrim A person who travels to a holy place.

Pioneer A person who goes where no one else has been before.

Skippered To have been the captain of a boat.

Spinster A woman who has never married.

Submissive Obedient, and tending to let other people decide what to do.

Synod A council of church officials.

Unconventional Breaking with the normal ways of society, such as in dress, behaviour and attitudes.

Uncultivated Not having been prepared or used for growing crops.

Womens' Liberation Movement An informal political movement, beginning in the 1960s, which through demonstrations, petitions and other means demanded equal rights for women.

Index

*Numbers in **bold** refer to illustrations.*